A Divorcee's Financial Survival Guide

A Divorcee's Financial Survival Guide

HOW TO INVEST YOUR
SETTLEMENT LIKE AN EXPERT

• • •

Lee Hyder

© 2017 Lee Hyder
All rights reserved.

ISBN: 1974582159
ISBN 13: 9781974582150

New Beginnings

• • •

IF YOU ARE READING THIS book, I don't know if I should congratulate you or say I am sorry or a little bit of both. Divorce is never easy, but in most cases it is a necessary evil. I know a little bit about this subject since I was married for almost twenty-five years and had been with my ex for almost thirty years by the time of our divorce.

I won't bore you with the details that led up to our divorce, but I will say that it exposed to me how little my ex really understood about investing. Her lack of investing knowledge, experience, and confidence created in her an incredible amount of fear and anxiety concerning how to properly invest her divorce settlement. My ex shared with me that she had no idea how to invest her settlement money. Now she needed to create investment strategies to be sure she wouldn't run out of money and her money would last her entire lifetime. This was my motivation in writing this book. I wanted to help other divorced women eliminate any fears and anxiety they may have concerning investing. I wanted to give them the necessary tools and confidence to help them navigate through the financial maze of investing decisions.

Investing is a lot more complicated than just buying "good investments"

Often when people interview financial advisers they are considering using, they usually focus on the wrong things and ultimately don't ask the pivotal questions they should. **This book will help you determine the most important questions to ask any prospective financial adviser you are considering using.** To make matters even worse, the time following a divorce can be a highly emotionally charged one, and during these times, people tend to make bad decisions. Dealing with your financial future is one place you need a clear head, free from emotion.

I understand that there's a large segment of women who can probably do a much better job managing and investing their money than their ex-husbands did. They may have even made most of the investment decisions during their marriage. If that's you, that's great, but keep reading because you'll still pick up some great strategies that maybe can help improve on your existing investing skills. If, on the other hand, you're like my ex-wife and are confronted with having to make 100 percent of the investment decisions on your own for the first time in a long time, this book will definitely help you take charge of your financial future and become more confident along the way.

If you think you were confused, scared, and frustrated during the divorce process, you haven't seen anything yet. Now that the fighting for your share of the money is over and the settlement that you received is safely tucked away in the bank or will be soon, get ready to be scared to death, and you should be. Why scared to death you say? When was the last time you had had to make a $200,000, $400,000, or larger single financial decision alone? Most will say "never." Now you do. If you do it right, both you and your family will have a great life, free from financial worry and sleepless nights. Do it wrong, and you can lose a lot of your money so quickly your head will spin.

I've been coaching northeast Ohio divorcées for almost twenty-five years on how to **protect, preserve,** and **invest their divorce settlements so they won't run out of money.** I have taught these strategies and philosophies at many of northeast Ohio local colleges and universities.

If you made all the day-to-day investing decisions in your home while you were married, you may not be overly concerned about handling your divorce settlement. In my twenty-five years of experience in advising divorcées, I have found that is not the rule but the exception for most divorcées.

Many divorcées have told me that in their previous married lives, they allowed their exes to handle all the day-to-day investing decisions. Even though they may have reviewed the investments from time to time with their exes, many divorcées admit they had little understanding of the true details of investing. For the most part, they didn't think that they needed to worry about the investing or running out of money during retirement; that was their husband's job.

Now you do! You may have counted on your ex-husband to take care of you concerning investing "till death do us part." It was understood that was his job. Now that you are divorced, it's 100 percent your job. Now you must figure how to find a financial coach you can trust and then make sure that

- whatever portfolio he or she designs for you is appropriate for your specific risk tolerance and time horizon;
- you are properly diversified with a well-balanced mix of both domestic and international holdings;
- you're not paying too much in needless fees;
- Portfolio turnover is kept to a minimum;
- you know how and when to rebalance your portfolio;
- your standard deviation isn't too high; and
- above everything else, there will be enough money to last your entire lifetime.

These are just a few of the new terms, ideas, and strategies this book will teach you while removing your fear concerning your financial future.

You may be saying to yourself how hard can all this investing stuff be? Today we have all those crazy Internet websites and talking heads on TV and radio shows shouting out their endless messages and beliefs that the stock market is predictable.

They want you to believe all you needed to do is whatever they are saying to do with your money, and your financial future is almost assured. And, of course, you could ask some of your other divorced friends how they invested their divorce settlements and just duplicate whatever they did. I'll come back to taking advice from friends later.

Most people today would scoff at a fortune-teller at a county fair, who predicted their future. Those same people accept lock, stock, and barrel stock predictions because they come from a well-known TV or radio anchor, website, or magazine.

This so-called objective, impersonal advice we get on TV, radio, or the Internet is dressed up and packaged as consumer education when it's nothing more than a fancy and expensive infomercial for whatever they are selling today. Sadly, for most divorcées, I feel their real education they long for comes too late after they bit on the apple and implemented all this impersonal advice from someone they don't even know. Worse yet, all these advice givers have no idea about your personal situation, wants, fears, financial needs, or risk tolerance.

I can't tell you the countless number of divorcées who would come into my office or call me wanting to buy something they saw on TV, heard about on the radio, or read somewhere. It is amazing the power that TV, radio, and the Internet have on people's minds, emotions, and investing decisions. I know what you're saying—not yours!

Emotions can be a wonderful gift, but investing needs to be one human activity we should leave our emotions out of. Throughout this book, I hope to identify many of these investing traps that are all around us and show you how you can avoid them. Once you recognize them, it will be much easier for you to come up with an investing philosophy and strategy that will help you make better decisions with your investments for your new life.

Size Doesn't Matter

• • •

OR AT LEAST THAT'S WHAT my editor said.

This book won't be long because it doesn't have to be to get my simple yet powerful points across to you.

I am going to share with you what I have learned over my twenty-five years of dealing both with portfolios and with the divorcées who have them.

Art Linkletter once said, "Kids say the darndest things." I will take artistic privilege and change that a little by saying "newly divorced women" do the darnedest things.

Who will benefit by reading this book?

If you are hoping this book will be full of charts, graphs, technical data, and secret stock tips that will make you rich overnight, you better read every page very carefully because you are already in danger of destroying your future retirement.

Many believe that to be a successful investor and get on track for a great retirement, all you need to do is the following:

1. Watch TV or listen to a radio show where the host barks out stock tips as casually as a waitress yells to a short-order cook, "Eggs over easy."
2. Subscribe to the newest newsletter promising you the greatest stock tips that can't miss.
3. Ask Google or any other website what's hot.
4. Buy or consider buying some overpriced educational or trading systems.
5. Rely on your custodian's magical online tools and research.
6. Believe that past performance of a mutual fund or stock is a pretty good indicator of how it will perform in the future.
7. Believe that the stock market is predictable and act accordingly.
8. Belong to an investing club.

9. Rely on Morningstar as the final authority for what to invest in.
10. Or best yet, just invest in whatever your other divorced friends do because you think your friends really know what they are doing!

A SERIOUS WARNING ABOUT TAKING WELL-MEANING INVESTING ADVICE FROM YOUR OTHER DIVORCED FRIENDS

To the outside world, your friends may appear as if they are successful investors and really know what there doing: They may have the big house, expensive car, and membership to "the club," and there always taking fun vacations. They seem to have it all. You may secretly even be a little jealous of their lives. **Be very careful what you wish for.**

I can't tell you how often I sit in front of divorced women who look great to the outside world. They certainly look like they have

it all, but after they share with me what's really going on financially, the real picture is much different from the one they portray to everyone else. Even though they came to my office in an expensive car, many of these women are in serious financial trouble and don't even know it. I can't believe how many divorcées walk into my office with $25,000 or more in credit-card debt, have stripped all their equity from their huge, well-manicured home, and that expensive car they drove to my office in has a huge payment and even have unnecessary loans they are saddled with. The irony of these sad situations is these women tend to be the most opinionated and eager to share their secrets about how you should invest your money. **Please be very careful from whom you take life-changing advice from.**

1 + 1 = 2 Maybe?

• • •

BEING A FINANCIAL ADVISER—SOMEONE WHO has dealt with numbers, math, graphs, charts, and formulas over my entire twenty-five-year professional career—how can I possibly say **1 + 1 = 2 maybe**?

First of all, not only will I demonstrate to you that this is true, but soon you will come to realize, like I have, that our entire economy is based on the simple truth that **1 + 1 = 2 maybe** or, said another way, "sometimes." What I am trying to say is, quite often, what we see with our own eyes and think we understand may actually be more complicated than we realize. The outcome that we believed to be so cut and dried may not be as predictable after all.

I first learned of this well-guarded secret almost fifty-five years ago, as a young child sitting around the kitchen table with my family. My father was a CPA. He liked to joke by saying that was an acronym for "cleaning, pressing, and alterations." I didn't think it was funny, but he always smiled when he said it.

I was always intrigued when my father would fill in endless numbers perfectly in column after column with those lead refill pencils that are almost impossible to find today. I remember looking over his shoulder and asking what he was doing. He would try to explain to me in CPA language that it was his job to try to help families reduce the amount of income tax they owed. I would ask this: If they owed it, how can you save them any money? That idea was foreign to this nine-year-old boy. Even I knew you owe what you owe.

As a nine-year-old, I needed a much simpler explanation, so my dad shared with me his secret formula: **1 + 1 = 2 maybe** or sometimes.

Not only would this simple mathematical example stay with me my entire life, but it would also become a foundational belief that guided me in helping countless divorcées achieve peace of mind as investors and, more importantly, help them better understand the world they live in. I guess what my dad was simply trying to say to me was that things may really not be as cut and dried as they appear to be.

Are you ready to learn this formula and see how it can affect your entire thought process over your entire lifetime if you're not careful?

Okay, here it is.

[handwritten mathematical formulas]

Let's say if you earn $50,000 of income at your job and you are, let's say, in a 30 percent tax bracket, your tax is $15,000. Simple math, isn't it?

Through the eyes of my dad, a CPA, he would say maybe you owe $15,000. His job was to find every legal loophole, deduction, credit, and offset to reduce your income and ultimately reduce your tax.

How many other countless industries and situations can you apply this philosophy to? How many other times did you see or hear something on TV or the radio or read something in a magazine, newspaper, or online that made sense to you at the time, so much so that the outcome seemed so predictable, only to be shocked by the ultimate outcome?

$1 + 1 = 2$ MAYBE.
Remember these sure bets?

- The Trump versus Clinton election
- Rodney King verdict
- O. J. Simpson verdict
- The dot-com era
- The real-estate bubble
- Maybe your own tax return

You may have your own list where, in your mind, the outcome of a situation or event was easily predictable—or so you thought, based on what you were being spoon-fed by outside influences. It's very hard for the average person to separate the wheat from the chaff. In the hands of a well-trained attorney, PR firm, media, or financial adviser with great charts and graphs, what appears to be 100 percent predictable cannot only shock you but also shock the entire world.

You may be asking yourself, what does this have to do with my divorce settlement and my investments?

Great question. My goal in writing this book is to demonstrate to you that Wall Street and all those other countless talking heads you watch on TV, listen to on the radio, or read online, in your newspaper, or in magazines, books, or journals have one job, and that's to convince you that all you need to do is take their advice, and the outcome is predictable.

Wouldn't that make investing simple if the stock market was really that predictable? Sure it would, but the stock market is not predictable. Don't look for some "financial fortune-teller" on TV, radio, or magazine or online to tell you what to do with your divorce settlement.

Learn this rule well, and you will learn how to defend yourself from falling prey to it and its dangerous consequences. As an investor, if you learn it well, it can help you make better investment decisions and steer clear from all the financial noise that can derail your financial future. With a little bit of luck, lots of discipline, and patience, you may make it to that beach and lounge chair in retirement after all.

When I first meet with new divorcées, all that they want to focus on is our portfolios' historical rates of return. I can understand that based on where the average investor is coming from and how little else they pay attention to. I get it: they want to compare what other advisers are saying their most recent returns are to ours as if that tells the entire story. Sadly, many investors believe it does.

In their minds, it's as if they are saying to themselves, "If our portfolios performed better than the other adviser's they are considering using, they may feel they should select us and have us manage their divorce settlement." On the other hand, if the other adviser's portfolio happened to outperform ours, then in their minds, they are obviously thinking that the other adviser is doing a better job and they should choose that adviser.

If you are a typical investor, you may be saying to yourself, "That makes sense to me." I guess on the surface it does, but **understanding investing and portfolio design requires a focus on more than simply last year's returns.**

Although I can't deny that we all want a great rate of return, **the rate of return alone only tells part of the story.** I believe all investors benefit by having very diversified portfolios. Further, I believe diversification should be found not just in the US markets but also in the international markets. In addition, **you want to be sure that you are not assuming any unnecessary risk** and, more importantly, you understand how much risk you are taking on and the consequences of it.

So what does risk and diversification have to do with our portfolios underperforming another adviser's portfolio?

First of all, rates of return vary from year to year. Even though our portfolios may have underperformed the other adviser's for a year or two, does that mean you should choose them over us?

Let's assume for the last two years, the other adviser's portfolio may have outearned our portfolios. The real question you should be asking yourself is why:

1. They probably have a higher equity allocation and are taking on way more risk than you are aware of. Even though that riskier allocation has produced a higher return, without a systematic rebalancing strategy, free from emotional decisions when the market swings the other way, then sadly, you will understand the

consequences of only focusing on achieving higher returns. Then you will learn the meaning of "risk-related return" the hard way. Everyone talks about a portfolio's upward returns, but few stop and do the same on the way down. We do. **We believe you need to have a strategy to protect your downside position, other than simply market timing.** That's what we do, and it starts and ends with the design, implementation, and management of the specific allocation we create for you. These allocations will help you achieve the returns in the range you want while keeping the volatility in the specific range that you can live with.

2. You may not accept this, but they probably just got lucky. There's no denying that luck can play a part in everyone's portfolio from time to time. As an adviser, I would much rather be disciplined and adhere to an academic philosophy than rely on luck. The hard part for many investors is knowing the difference.
3. Their portfolio wasn't as diversified as ours. Now I am sure you are saying, "Who cares? They beat your return."

Let me share with you what's probably going on by giving you a real-life example.

If you recall, 2014 was not a great year for the US market except for the S&P 500/US large caps, which were up around 14 percent. Some of our portfolios may only have a maximum of only 10 percent in US large-cap stocks in our most aggressive allocations. That means if you were a fifty-fifty investor with a $100,000 portfolio, you would have 50 percent, or $50,000, in equities and 50 percent, or $50,000, in fixed income. Our fifty-fifty allocation only has 4 percent in US large caps, which means of your $50,000 in equities, only $2,000 is in the US large caps, which yielded 14 percent. In this example, only $2,000 out of your entire $50,000 earned 14 percent. Now you can at least understand why, in 2014, our portfolios were flat across most allocations.

On the other hand, if you made money in 2014, I believe you were not only lucky but ill-advised because you clearly had most of your money in the S&P 500/large caps and didn't have a diversified portfolio. You may be saying to yourself, "So what? My portfolio made money, and yours didn't."

In my opinion, if you made money in 2014, you may want to consider firing your adviser. Why would I fire my adviser, you ask, if he made me money, when everyone else didn't? The reason why you may want to fire your adviser is because he or she had way too much of your money in any one US asset class—US large caps just happened to be the only US asset class to make money that year. Luck or skill—you tell me. If it was luck, and I don't know anything else you can call it, do you really want your adviser to believe in luck as a strategy, or do you want to use sound academic principles?

So, in this case, being globally diversified as we are did not help us for 2014, but I wouldn't change a thing in our portfolio design. The problem is, you probably wouldn't either, and that's actually the bigger issue.

History shows us time and time again that past performance is no guarantee of future performance. I would always recommend a well-diversified portfolio over having most of your money in any one particular asset class.

There's always a reason why one portfolio outearns another portfolio. The real trick is knowing why.

Successful Investing Is a Lot like Religion and Faith

• • •

NOW THAT I HAVE YOUR attention—and if you haven't tossed the book across the room yet—let me explain what I mean. I am not talking about any specific religion. I am referring to simply having faith. When I say faith, I am referring to something that you believe in and can rely and lean on when the going gets tough in your life. Let me give you an example.

Life has a way of knocking us all down from time to time. It can be your recent divorce, an unexpected death of a spouse, the unthinkable death of a child, a drug or alcohol addiction, or the loss of a job. You get the idea. No matter who we are or how much money we have or don't have, tragedy can and does strike all walks of life from the bus driver to the famous movie star or athlete. The real question is this: When we are suddenly faced with this crisis, how do we handle it?

I believe we all have personally witnessed people who have been faced with many of these life challenges and have witnessed these people who have handled the same situations so differently.

Quite often the families that have a religious background, what I call "faith," will still have the same emotional issues to deal with and work through, but their faith will help them survive these stressful times without a dysfunctional and destructive response and by not destroying their lives and others around them as well.

We also have either personally observed or known of other people who have had similar crises but had no religious background or faith, and they handled the situation very differently. They may have turned to alcohol, drugs, gambling, isolation, or worse. Their lack of faith had serious consequences affecting them and others.

So what does this have to do with investing?

I believe if you have taken the time to develop a true philosophy about investing—one based on sound academic principles over time, not just a hunch or what one talking head says on TV or chasing last year's winners—this financial faith will help you avoid making dangerous emotional, and often self-destructive, decisions about your portfolio.

On the other hand, **if you really haven't taken the time to develop a true investing philosophy, one that you can live with in both good and bad times, you may be in danger of using a follow-the-leader approach to investing**. That's simply buying or selling what everyone is talking about. If this describes the approach that makes sense to you, then you may be in real danger of blowing up your retirement and losing your divorce settlement to the stock market in the future.

Sadly enough, this group comprises the largest segment of investors on Wall Street. The media makes it even worse by yelling, "Fire," "Sell, sell, sell," "Run to cash," or "The danger has passed, and it's okay to get back into the market again." TV, radio, and other media are great at creating the stampede both out of the market and back to it as well.

My hope is that this book will help you develop a simple philosophy about investing that will guide you throughout your pre- and post-retirement years. In addition, it will help you make better investing decisions about the divorce settlement you fought so hard to get in the first place. It should also help you avoid getting trampled to death as the pundits shout, "Sharks! Get out of the water!" as you wait patiently on the water's edge for the all-safe whistle to get back in.

One of the Most Important Questions You Need to Ask Yourself about Investing

• • •

WHAT DO YOU BELIEVE ABOUT MARKETS, AND WHERE DO RETURNS REALLY COME FROM?

WHAT I AM SIMPLY ASKING you is this: **Do you believe the stock market is predictable? Yes or no?** Do you believe all those talking heads on TV and radio who tell us what to buy and sell really know the future? After all, isn't that what they are really saying or selling, I should say?

Most people would be very quick to say, "Of course, I don't." Given the opportunity to do a portfolio analysis on your current investments, I would probably find that if you are like most investors, the analysis would tell a completely different story.

If most investors don't think the stock market is predictable, then explain to me why most investors come into my office with portfolios that are incredibly underdiversified? Quite often, a very large percentage of their US equity is mostly, if not entirely, invested in the S&P 500/large-cap stocks. Worse yet, they have little if any money in US small or small-value companies, let alone any investments overseas.

**You say and even believe that you don't think
the stock market is predictable
but what you may actually be doing with your investments could shout out
a completely different story.**

If that's you, here's an easy fix.

Just stop saying you don't think the market is predictable, or change what you are doing.

All I am asking you to do is be sure what you are saying is truly in alignment with what you are doing.

You may not think that you have an investment philosophy or strategy, but the way your portfolio is designed says at least your adviser does. Don't you think it would be a good idea for both you and your adviser to be on the same page and have the same philosophy?

It would be almost comical when people bantered around investment conversation and advice every day to each other—if the consequences weren't so dire.

> **People are so quick to repeat what they heard today about the stock market, and they have zero understanding of how what they heard will or will not affect their personal portfolios.**

Let me give you an easy example. A divorcée may walk into my office wanting investment advice while the S&P 500 or the Dow is struggling and say something like the market and the economy are having a difficult time lately. When I ask her to define for me what she calls "the market," it's clear to me that she believes the stock market is simply the S&P 500 and the Dow, without paying any attention to the additional US asset classes, let alone the rest of the world's investing opportunities.

> **How can anyone hope to achieve "market returns" when all they invest in are the S&P 500/large-cap stocks or the Dow or just in the United States?**

On the other hand, I would define "the market" completely differently. My definition would also include markets outside the United States, not simply the S&P 500 and the Dow.

When you examine our portfolios, our global view of investing and diversification is clearly reflected in them and their design. The portfolios that we tailor for you look very different, with much more worldwide diversification than what most people have when they come into our office.

If you recall, we said earlier that for many people who come to our office and allow us to do a portfolio analysis of their current investments, most of their US funds are in US large caps/S&P 500. Many may have as much as 60 percent or more of their US investments in US large caps. In contrast, many of our portfolios will have less than 10 percent of all US equity in US large caps. This allows us to have more of an investor's funds still available to be invested in more diversified ways in the United States and overseas. We also find these same people who may have some money invested overseas also have most if not all of their money in the overseas equivalent of US large caps, ignoring international diversification.

A Few Simple Investing Rules to Follow

• • •

THESE RULES OF INVESTING ARE simple but not that easy to follow. You could probably say the same thing about dieting. The rules for losing weight are to eat less and move more.

I believe the rules to investing are equally easy to understand but just as hard to follow.

Own equities. I believe equities are the greatest way to create wealth known to humankind. When you invest in equities, you are investing in the free enterprise system. Even though half the civilized population loves their iPhones, I am fairly confident that somewhere in the free world there is some company trying to invent a new cell phone, gadget, or product that hopes to one-up the competition, and if successful, they will be handsomely rewarded for their effort. Maybe it will happen, maybe it won't, but when this no-name company is ready to go public, the world will decide if its new product or invention is worth investing in. This story plays itself out thousands of times a year throughout the free world. It did with Apple, Facebook, and Google, just to mention a few. As long as there are people with dreams and new visions, there will be equities to invest in and people who profit by wisely doing so. Of course, the real secret is determining which ones to invest in and which ones to pass on.

Be diversified. Invest all over the world and in many different asset classes. We live in a global economy, and long gone are the days when a prudent investor can say they want market returns and still has all or most of their investments in the United States.

Have a systematic plan to rebalance on the highs and lows that will take emotion out of the equation. When I ask investors when and why they rebalance, it's apparent they don't have a true understanding or a systematic plan to do so or why you even do it in the first place. Most just wing it at best. **Rebalancing is not as much about trying to increase your return as it is being sure that your portfolio doesn't drift from your specific desired allocation preference to a more risky one. Let's assume you choose to be a fifty-fifty investor.** That's 50 percent in equities of some kind and 50 percent in fixed income and bonds. You chose this fifty-fifty allocation because the risk and volatility were explained to you, and as much as you wanted to attempt to earn a higher rate of return, you weren't comfortable with a higher equity allocation and taking on more risk. Let's assume your 50 percent equity position goes up 10 percent. Do you rebalance back to fifty-fifty? Of course not. You just earned 10 percent, but suddenly you have drifted to a fifty-five-forty-five allocation. Luckily again, your 55 percent equity continues to inch its way up, and again, it gains another 10 percent. Now you have drifted to an approximately 60 percent equity and 40 percent fixed income allocation. Do you rebalance back to your original fifty-fifty? Heck no. You're invincible and on autopilot, and greed has its hooks deeply embedded in you. Simply put, which allocation—fifty-fifty, sixty-forty, or seventy-thirty—is riskier and has much more volatility? A seventy-thirty, of course. Eventually, the market drops, and you get hammered and look for someone to blame.

How could this significant, needless loss have been avoided? Simple. If you'd had a systematic strategy to rebalance, free from emotion, your portfolio wouldn't have drifted to seventy-thirty in the first place. For example, I recommend you review the portfolio quarterly; if the portfolio allocation has drifted by more than 5 percent up or down, I would advise to rebalance back to the target allocation. Of course, you don't have to use a 5 percent per quarter strategy, but committing to having a number and a system takes the emotion and guesswork out of it.

Be sure all your investments aren't highly correlated the same. When you design and construct your portfolio, you want to be sure that all your investments are not highly correlated alike. You don't want your entire portfolio to move in the same direction at the same time.

Pay attention to fees. Size matters, especially in the fees that you're paying. One of the fastest ways you may be able to increase your returns is by reducing the fees you're paying. If you have no idea what you're paying in true overall fees, how can you go shopping for something with lower fees? You can't!

It still surprises me that many divorcées say, "I don't worry about the fees. I just look at the bottom line." They also may say something like, "I'm happy with my returns. I made 9 percent last year." The truth is, they may have made a lot more than 9 percent, but that's what they were able to keep after all the fees came out. They may have made 12 percent but had 3 percent in fees. If that's the case, try to find an investment replacement in the same sector with less fees. It really amazes me that **most people know what they paid per gallon of gas last week to the penny but really have no idea what they are paying in investment fees**. That's simply not okay anymore!

There are many different fees you may be paying, and some you may not even know exist. Of course, there are the **adviser's fees,** but those are usually found on your statements. There are additional fees that are almost impossible to find, and, if you believe Wall Street, they don't even matter. **Some of these fees include the expense ratio on mutual funds, 12b-1 fees, portfolio turnover fees, and front- and back-end loads.**

If you are saying to yourself that you have never heard of any of these fees and have no idea if you are paying any of them, that's a problem.

Don't gamble on hot picks or anything trendy. Buying trendy clothes or electronics may be fun, but try to avoid buying into a trend concerning your investments. I know doing so can feel like the cool thing to do, but **you need to know the difference between gambling and speculating with your money** and prudent investing that has the broad backing of academics to support your investment decisions.

Be disciplined, and stay the course. Delbar is a research group out of Boston that tracks investors' behaviors and results. Delbar finds that **the average investor not only significantly underperforms the market but does so often because he or she changes and tinkers with their portfolio about every three years**. Think about that. The average person reading this (and yes, I know, that's not you—you're not average!) is more committed to wearing their worn-down shoes longer than in sticking with the investment decisions they made less than four years ago. How scary is that?

Avoid market timing. Market timing is getting in the market because you believe that it's a great time to invest or getting out because you think it's time to sell. **Market timing can destroy a retirement.** If this is your philosophy, the problem is that you have to be right twice every time you do this—once when you get out and once when you decide to get back in. If you time the market, for example, ten times a year, that's ten times getting out of the market and ten times eventually getting back in. That's twenty times per year, and if you are going to do that as a philosophy over a forty-five-year investing career, you only have to be right about nine hundred times. Good luck with that! **Studies show some of the market's greatest upticks immediately follow some of the biggest market drops.** Most people who market-time miss all or most of that upward bounce because they're still sitting on the sidelines.

Remember that past performance isn't any guarantee of future performance. This is so widely understood that when I teach retirement classes at some of the local universities, I will start by saying this well-known-but-not-believed phrase and, without fail, the entire class will all jump in and complete it for me. You may be saying it to yourself right now. Study after study shows that a manager's past performance has no correlation with his or her future performance, but **the average investor still wants to look in the rearview mirror to pick investments.** *Don't do it!*

Remember that no one can predict the future. And if they could, would they really tell you? Let me repeat this: no one can predict what's going to happen in the stock market today, tomorrow, next week, or next year. No TV or radio host shouting what to buy, no newspaper, Internet website, or your smart friend. No one!

Know how to measure volatility in your portfolio. Not all risk is the same. You shouldn't take any more risk than necessary to achieve the return you are after. **One of the most important numbers you should know concerning your portfolio is its** *standard deviation.* In simple terms, it's a number that each stock and mutual fund has. When you combine all these different stocks and funds into a comprehensive portfolio, they all interact with each other, and this creates a new standard deviation for the entire portfolio. **The higher the standard deviation, the higher the expected return may be in good times, and it reveals how much downward volatility you should expect in bad times.**

Knowing your standard deviation is that critical to your long-term financial health. It may possibly reduce your standard deviation and either keep your return the same or possibly increase it. **Do you know your standard deviation?** If you knew that your standard deviation was too high in 2007, and you reduced it, you might not have lost nearly as much in the 2008 crash.

All I Want to Do Is Beat the S&P 500

• • •

TODAY EVERY INVESTOR'S MAIN FOCUS is trying to beat the S&P 500, as if the S&P 500 is the holy grail of investing—or that's at least what the media has convinced us we should want as our investing goal. Perhaps that may explain why so many portfolios we review are so heavily invested in it.

Every mutual fund's ultimate trophy to hold high on January 1 is one reflecting that the fund beat the S&P 500. What a powerful advertisement or headline to lure you to roll the dice and invest with the fund, hoping it can beat the S&P 500 again next year. What makes the fund so special? Nothing.

Stop and ask yourself a simple question.

Are the fund managers reporting history, what has happened last year, or what will happen next year? Last year, of course. Not one of these firms that have graced the covers of countless magazines, newsletters, and other media, bragging about beating the S&P 500 last year, will ever dare to make a prediction that one of their many funds will do it again this year.

Imagine if you were a meteorologist, and your boss came in and said, "If your weather forecast isn't 100 percent accurate today, you will lose your job." Wow, that's a lot of pressure, especially living in Cleveland. That task sounds impossible to do, doesn't it? Maybe not. How about if the boss continued and said, "Today I want your forecast to simply report on yesterday's weather." Now the task got much easier, didn't it?

So how does Wall Street convince us that all you have to do is follow their advice and success is almost assured?

The Law of Large Numbers

• • •

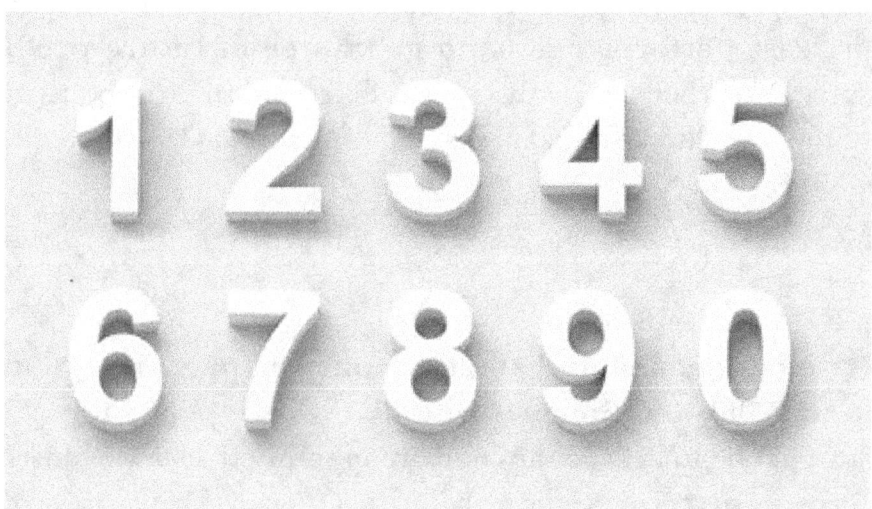

IF YOU ARE A MUTUAL-FUND family that has literally hundreds of different funds to choose from, how do you convince investors to buy your funds? Beat the S&P 500 last year, and investors will beat a path to your door this year.

If the goal is to simply beat the S&P 500, isn't there a 50 percent chance of success? You either beat it or don't. Let's assume your family of funds has five hundred different funds for investors to choose from. I am not a mathematician, but even I know that if there are five hundred funds and I have a 50 percent chance, I would expect anywhere between two hundred and three hundred or maybe more of these five hundred funds to beat the S&P 500. No magic or special skill there—just the law of large numbers. **The real magic is how easily these mutual funds can share last year's results to investors and you assume that these funds managers are so special that all you will need to do to achieve financial success is invest in last year's winners.**

Who cares that for years we have been told over and over again that…get ready, I know you are already saying the words to yourself: **"Past performance is no guarantee of future performance."** Yes, but you say this time is different, isn't it? No, it's not!

Stop trying to beat the market, and start trying to achieve market returns.

Stop Trying to Beat the Market

It's well documented that most money managers can't beat the S&P 500, and the ones who do rarely repeat. My goal for you would be to help you think more in terms of achieving market returns versus trying to beat the market. Again, Delbar is a company that tracks investors' results and behaviors, and its research has indicated that most investors underperform the market. In addition, **there is a big difference between what the specific investment earns and what the investor earns.** What did I say? You read that right—most investors don't earn what the market yields. It's as if the market knocks on your front door and says, "We are going to yield eight percent this year. Would you like to earn eight percent?" To which you say, "No, I am fine doing it my way and following my own hunches. Typically, the result is you earn less than the market.

How does this happen? It's mostly due to investor behaviors.

Didn't I Hear This Somewhere Before?
Yes, you did!

I know we reviewed these points before, but they are so critical to an investor's success that they are worth repeating.

Investors change all or part of their portfolios too often. If designed properly, your specific investment strategy should help guide you throughout your entire life as an investor and keep you from making these needless and frequent changes.

Track-record investing. Even though we know the rules, investors get sucked in and use the past performance of an investment heavily to influence their future investment decisions.

Stock picking. Too many investors spend countless hours trying to find magical stocks that they believe will forever change their portfolio for the better. Stop looking.

Market timing. Here's another area I know most investors would agree with but have a very difficult time living with. Market timing is simply getting into (or out of) the market. Market timing is dangerous and so destructive, so please avoid it at all costs.

> **These are all investor behavioral issues and not actual portfolio issues, but clearly your behavior will affect your portfolio results.**

US Large Caps, Aisle 4

• • •

To the average investor, investing is nothing more than shopping for things that you believe are a good investment.

Sounds easy enough. Duh, you say—but not so quickly. Really. What do you think the average investor looks for when making investment decisions? As much as I rail against it, **I still find that 90 percent of all people I talk to tell me that they look at how**

well it has done in the past. They pay zero attention to the standard deviation of their portfolio, fees, turnover, or overlap, nor do they know the importance of these terms. Do you?

It's as if people think that by filling up their shopping cart with good past-performing investments, whatever those may be, they are assured a great portfolio return in the future. That's no truer than saying if you pick up good food at the market, you are assured a great meal. Who needs a stinking recipe? Who cares about using way too much salt? I hope you are not part of the crowd saying, "I don't see a problem yet."

HERE'S THE PROBLEM.

No one has just one stock or one mutual fund as their portfolio. At least, I hope not.

As you fill your shopping cart with investments, do you have the slightest idea how the different investments will all work together?

Are they all highly correlated the same? I hope not; how noncorrelated are they or should they be? Do you know the total amount of combined fees, overlap, and turnover or standard deviation you have in the entire portfolio? If you look for international investments, and I hope you do, what countries will you look for, and which are the ones to avoid? How will you determine the proper percentage of each? And what about rebalancing? **These are just some of the big problems that most investors don't pay a lot of attention to. Do you?**

When we design and engineer a portfolio, it is more than simply the sum of all investments. A good portfolio is engineered and designed to work together with the tens of thousands of holdings from all over the world in many different asset classes. That's what comprises a diversified portfolio. This is what is missing from and is critical to most do-it-yourself investors and their portfolios.

How do you make your investment decisions? When I ask average investors how they make investment decisions, again 90 percent will say to me that they look at the following:

- What it earned last year
- What it has averaged over the last five and ten years

For most people, that's it.

In my opinion, those are two of the most worthless pieces of information you could look at when making your investment choices.

Recall what I shared earlier:

1. Past performance has no bearing on future returns.

2. According to Delbar, most people tinker or change their investments every three years, so how does a five- or ten-year average even help you?

Remember that the published five- and ten-year returns only go to the few disciplined investors who don't change their investments over that five- and ten-year time period. If you are average, and I hope you aren't, you aren't even earning what the investment has yielded. Most investors don't.

There's normally an incredible difference between what the investment itself has earned and what you, the investor, earns. The investment is committed for the long term and disciplined, but most investors aren't and can't say the same thing. That's why we said earlier that while most investors are busy trying to beat the market, they usually underperform it time and time again.

I believe an investor should be more concerned about the following questions:

1. What is this investment designed to earn (average) over the next ten to twenty years? **(if they're willing to learn how to be a disciplined investor)**
2. What is my expected downside risk that I should expect to lose occasionally if the market goes south? (And it will over time, so knowing this number is critical.) **Can you say "standard deviation"?**

The financial industry tries at all costs to stay away from the word "guarantee." Many advisers I know have gotten into trouble from the mere mention of that word. Regulators go to painstaking efforts to be sure advisers don't cite returns in literature or on their websites or marketing materials. They want to protect investors from being led to believe past performance somehow has any bearing on future returns. **The sad thing is that's exactly what most investors rely on.** Here's something I can guarantee and will sleep well knowing: no regulator will knock on my door because I used the following statement: "There will be periods of time your portfolio may perform way better than you ever thought it would, and you will think I am a genius. And, of course, there will be times that your portfolio will underperform your expectations, and you may wonder if I even know what I am doing."

Portfolio ups and downs are natural, common, and to be expected. When the leaves fall off your trees in October and November, you don't call your landscaper and scream at him to cut them down. There is a season for everything, and your investments are no different.

Here is the problem: if you are like most investors, you have no understanding of the actual downside potential of your portfolio. Why should you? Few advisers ever explain it to you while painting a pretty picture of the average returns that you may never see.

So, to me, the most critical piece of information you should focus on is finding the specific percentage of loss in any year in your portfolio that you can tolerate. Design your portfolio for that range of loss or close as possible, and don't make any changes other than to rebalance your portfolio. Once we can isolate that number, we can get back into the expected rate of return you can expect based on the amount of volatility you can live with. This is a realistic way to be sure you are designing a portfolio specifically built for your personal risk tolerance.

For me to be an effective adviser, I need you to say to me out loud the actual percentage of potential loss you can tolerate and not feel the necessity to alter your portfolio. I want to avoid words like "conservative" and "moderate," as a gauge to determine your risk tolerance because they mean different things to different people.

Take this easy test with a friend or family member to determine if you and your financial adviser are speaking the same language.

Let's assume you and your friends are all in the same moderate portfolio. You hear on the news that the stock market has gone down 30 percent. Write down, without sharing your answer, what percentage you would expect your portfolio to go down by as well.

Now compare the answers. I'll bet each person has a different percentage of loss. How can that be? We all are in the same moderate portfolio. We all experience the same 30 percent stock-market loss.

We all have a different definition of "moderate."

That's why I don't use industry language to determine your risk tolerance. That's why I asked you to tell me what percentage you can live with as an occasional downside; then we do the math against your portfolio and see if you still feel the same way.

Currently, most clients and advisers aren't even speaking the same language. How can we possibly hope to get on the same page with your adviser concerning your expectations?

Education Is Key

• • •

OFTEN WHEN A DIVORCÉE COMES in to meet with me, she will tell me that when she was married, she and her husband had changed advisers numerous times over the years. No matter who they worked with over the years, the outcome always seemed to be the same. She would often ask me "What makes me and my firm any different?"

I will patiently and politely retrace all that they had done over the years with the other advisers. I will listen carefully to what strategy they chose to use, what they did when there was volatility in the market, and what their thoughts were on rebalancing, fees, and risk.

Most of the time, I get a blank stare, and they would recite what sounds good, and hoped it makes them sound like they know what they are talking about. Ultimately, I smile and say, "It looks like the only common denominator with all the past advisers was you and your ex!"

Quite often, I believe the investors are a big part of the problem. They get bombarded with way too much information and have no investment philosophy but have unrealistic expectations, but they know that they want higher returns and will buy and sell as often as necessary to achieve them. Even if it means breaking the rules we reviewed earlier in the book.

Until investors get a handle on what they believe about the market and where returns come from, until they come up with a philosophy they can live with in both good and bad times, and until they understand how to measure risk and fees, they simply are stuck with making emotional and dangerous investment decisions.

**Our feelings, right or wrong,
will ultimately drive our investment decisions.**

If I, as a wealth coach, can't help you get clear on where you believe returns come from and help you develop a philosophy about returns and the market, I am destined to be the next adviser who will also disappoint you.

I can't stop anyone from watching or listening to any investment TV or radio show and reading any magazine or newspaper. This financial pornography floods the airwaves, newsstands, mailboxes, and computer screens and poisons the minds of many investors. This overload of information plants seeds of frustration, discontentment, and unrealistic expectations in people's minds about their portfolios.

If you are not careful, the next phone call you may make may be to your adviser with instructions to sell and buy based on what you heard on the latest TV show or something you just read.

Coaching Makes the Difference

• • •

OFTEN, ANYONE TRYING TO ACCOMPLISH something meaningful and significant needs a relationship with a coach. Coaching helps get you to the next level to achieve the accomplishments you seek. Most great athletes who are at the top of their game have many different kinds of coaches. Great business icons also use coaches. Today many people use life coaches. A good coach will help you achieve what you say you want to attain. A great coach can help bring an unemotional perspective to the task. A great coach will hold you accountable and not accept your excuses. A great coach will tell you what you need to hear but may not want to listen to.

I Can't Eat Any More

• • •

HAVE YOU EVER GONE ON a vacation and stayed at one of those fancy hotels that have an incredibly overpriced Sunday buffet? After you decide to spend fifty-nine dollars on a brunch, you walk into a ballroom that is filled with food from wall to wall. Where do you start? There are way too many choices. All you really wanted was breakfast.

It has become that way with investing information. There are more financial TV and radio shows than anyone would think is even possible. Worse yet, they air 24-7. Don't get me started with how much worthless information is packaged online or on TV or the radio as education. It is nothing more than a commercial or a fancy sales pitch just to sell you something.

Today you are being convinced to manage your own money online and use the many fun online tools and research. How hard can it be?

Research has shown that people with self-directed online trading accounts needlessly trade and speculate way more often than those without online trading accounts.

In addition, the newest trend is the so-called Robo advisers. You simply turn your financial future over to an online electronic robot, and it does all the investing for you. Now that sounds scary. I don't know about you, but I am certainly not comfortable handing over your entire divorce settlement to a computer. Are you?

Estate Planning 101

• • •

THE BEST FINANCIAL PLANS MAY be rendered worthless if you don't have a good estate plan in place. I need to say from the outset that I am not an attorney and that none of what I am about to share is intended to be legal advice in any way. The purpose of this section is to simply share with you what my professional career has exposed me to and to offer twenty-five years of experience in dealing with both attorneys and people's estates. I would recommend that if I say anything that hits home, seek legal advice.

What's an estate?

Everything you own is your estate, including your home, cars, stocks, bonds, mutual funds, cash, jewelry, and lawn mower.

What's an estate plan?

An estate plan is created to handle your possessions upon your death or disability.

You may be surprised to learn that many divorcées haven't even given any thought about changing their wills, power of attorneys, or even beneficiaries. Even scarier, many of them didn't even have any of these critical documents even while they were happily married. Let me walk you through some different situations, terms, ideas, and strategies you may want to explore with your attorney.

I have a will. What else do I need?

Having an up-to-date will drafted by an attorney from the state you live in is a great start. So many of the divorcées I meet with tell me that they don't have a will, or if they do, it's very old and hasn't been changed since her divorce. You always want to be sure that it is current and reflects your up-to-date wishes and situation now that you are divorced. It should be drafted by an attorney and be based on the law in the state you call your primary residence. A will isn't a valid or a working document until after you die. Be sure you and your heirs know where the original document is because often your heirs need to file the original will with the court. Many courts will not accept a copy.

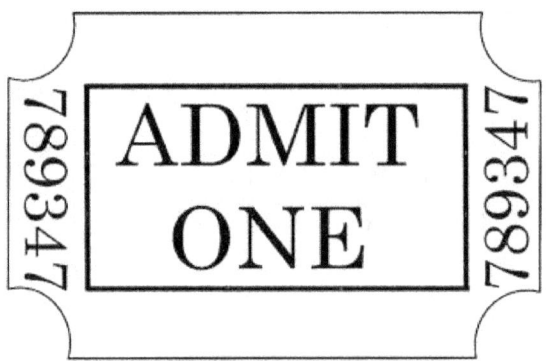

Your will is your ticket to probate.
Many people want to avoid probate and have their estates pass to heirs as fast as possible, with the fewest delays and least amount of expense. Many families have their wills drafted specifically to avoid probate without understanding that the wills they had drawn up may force them into the very long probate process they sought to avoid. **You may want to talk to your attorney about having**

a living trust rather than a conventional will as your main estate-planning document. Simply put, a revocable living trust normally will help you pass your estate to the heirs without all the delay and added cost of probate.

Many people don't want to give the entire estate to a heir all at once. If you find yourself not comfortable passing what took you a lifetime to achieve all at once, talk to your attorney about how a trust may be able to do a better job for you. One of the unique things about a trust is that you can design a custom lifelong distribution plan for beneficiaries to be paid out over time versus all at once.

I would recommend you have both a power of attorney for health care and a durable power of attorney. Many divorcées I talk to are still working, and their largest investment often is their 401(k)/403(b) or IRA in addition to their investments they got from the divorce settlement. These same families are often shocked when I tell them that if they don't have a durable power of attorney, and they become sick and are not able to function or conduct business, the caretaker or children won't able to get a penny from the 401(k), IRA, or 403(b) to help mom out.

Well, that's not entirely true. If you find yourself in this position, you will need to hire an attorney, go to the court, and have someone you trust apply to be the guardian so he or she can access these accounts under court supervision. This can be an expensive and time-consuming process. Having a durable power of attorney can prevent this outcome.

A *living will* is called many different things in different states, but it helps your family know your personal wishes concerning life and death and what kind of medical heroics you are willing to be subjected to. This simply makes it easier for the family, at a highly emotional time, to feel that they are not imposing their beliefs and decisions about prolonging your care. It further helps the family avoid getting into an emotional war over your deathbed. I have seen the aftermath of situations where the family didn't have this critical document to guide them and was forced to make decisions concerning the care of a loved one as the end drew closer. Often siblings took different positions. The damage this causes to the fabric of the family may never be able to be repaired.

Many people think that you must have a lot of money to be bothered with setting up an estate plan.

That's a common misconception.

The decision to set up an estate plan should not be solely based on how much money you have or don't have but, more importantly, also on how you feel about the

money you do have and that your family will inherit. It's kind of the opposite of what you may think as to who may benefit more by setting up an estate plan. The families who are lucky enough to have a lot of money can actually afford to go through the more expensive probate process, while the families that are less financially well-off may benefit more in protecting every dollar from probate. If I now have you thinking more about your estate plan and wanting to talk to your attorney, that's a good thing.

But what if you end up in a nursing home?

Now that that man you counted on till "death do us apart" is gone, you better have a plan B. If you don't invest some time and energy thinking about what could happen financially to you and your family if you end up in a nursing home, "it will probably end badly."

> It's paradoxical that the idea of living a long life appeals to everyone, but the idea of getting old doesn't appeal to anyone.
> —Andy Rooney

We all know that life isn't infinite and the grim reaper of death, disabilities, and despair won't be defeated. And while modern medicine has made huge strides in fighting heart disease, diabetes, and cancer, we all still die.

The lucky ones will die suddenly. Here today, living life to the fullest, gone tomorrow. Sad for our loved ones, but much better than dying a slow death, where our health declines daily, limited to a wheelchair, incapable of recalling our children's names, and needing assistance to visit the bathroom.

Depressing, isn't it? That's life.

As a society, we are living longer. That is a good thing, but that also means our money must last longer. It means that eventually we will become weak and likely to need help with those things we only want to do for ourselves (custodial care).

Here are some interesting statistics:

- If you reach age sixty-five, there's a 70 percent chance you'll need custodial care.
- The average nursing-home stay is almost three years.
- The average nursing-home cost is $70,000 a year.
- Nursing-home costs rise at twice the average inflation rate.
- Medicare doesn't pay for long-term care.
- Medicaid is available only after you've spent down your assets.
- Most people in nursing homes are on Medicaid, but they didn't start there.

Basically, you have three options when it comes to long-term care:

- **First, you can self-insure** and pay the nursing-home bill from your savings and investments. Perhaps you have enough money to do that. Remember, its $70,000 a year now. At 6 percent inflation, the price will double in twelve years. If you're married, and you get sick, will that leave enough money for your healthy spouse?

- **Second, you can't rely on Medicaid.** Why not? Most do, but that's available only after you've spent down your own money. If you're married, Medicaid kicks in when you have about $100,000 left. You don't have to sell your house, but the government may attach a lien to it after you die so that it can recoup the cost of your care.
- **Third, you can buy long-term-care insurance.** For many people, this is the right choice. Often, we hear people say they won't buy it out of fear they'll never use it and thus waste their money. We're going to let you in on a little secret: the people who go to nursing homes with long-term care don't win the game. It's those who have long-term-care insurance but die peacefully in their sleep—healthy today, dead tomorrow—who win the game.

    When your car isn't stolen, do you regret paying auto insurance? Never feel regret for being prudent.

Long-term-care insurance can be expensive, but a few things can be done to reduce it:

1. Limit coverage to four or five years. Odds are very high you won't need the policy after four years. By limiting coverage to this time frame, you reduce the cost dramatically over a lifetime-benefit policy.

2. Self-insure a part of the cost. If nursing homes in your area cost $200 per day, consider coverage for $150. Be sure to study the long-term impact of not being fully insured.
3. Ask your children to pay for it. They are the ones who stand to benefit from you not spending their inheritance on nursing-home care. Good luck with this one. A more realistic idea may be to ask the kids to help with some of the cost of long-term-care insurance.

Whatever you do, have a plan, and a plan isn't the kids will take care of me!

Closing Thoughts and Takeaways

• • •

TO HELP DIVORCÉES DEAL WITH this constant explosion of too much self-serving information that floods the air waves 24-7, I have created a series of ongoing "Coaching" educational classes for my clients. These classes are designed to help my clients deal with this information overload and give them current and accurate academic information about the market that is delivered without emotion or trying to scare them into some kind of dysfunctional investing behavior. **These classes help my clients become better**

informed and more educated investors. I attempt to act as a counterbalance to the endless financial misinformation and help them not overreact to the latest financial news story of the day.

For an invitation to any of my future classes in Akron, access to my online resources, or to receive my newsletter please e-mail me at lee@leehyder.com or go to www.leehyder.com

It's Not as Easy as It May Look.
There's more to designing a portfolio than just buying stocks and mutual funds, even if those stocks and funds have a great historical track record. (Remember what I said about track-record investing.)

Regardless of what you may think, read, and hear on TV or the radio, investing is not as easy as the media or big stock-brokerage firms would like you to believe. Even more important than determining what you should invest in is maintaining discipline throughout your investing career and keeping your emotions out of the equation.

Even if you could magically snap your fingers and have the perfect portfolio—if there is such a thing—if you are not truly disciplined and emotion free, you can destroy your perfect investment. I know that you are thinking, "Lee, that's not me. I am disciplined and didn't panic back in 2008."

Congratulations, but my experience tells me time and time again that if we really examine people's past investment decisions, we will find countless occasions where they acted more from a place of fear or greed, a hunch, or past performance than from an academic, well-defined, and disciplined strategy.

Many of you reading this may have, at one time or another, had a portfolio that was doing great, chugging along, and something happened. You panicked, and you reacted—maybe even overreacted—and changed something in your investment mix.

Of course, you wouldn't ever say that you overreacted. That change, in your mind, may appear to be very insignificant, but it was enough to alter the mix of asset classes in the portfolio, and now you may underperform the actual long-term return of the very investment you were in. Maybe had you just rebalanced the portfolio, you may have achieved the actual long-term return of the investment versus shooting yourself in your foot, just like Delbar says most investors do. Worse yet, you didn't even know it.

This is why most investors benefit by having a wealth coach versus a traditional adviser or stockbroker. Stockbrokers and many advisers do a good job in selling you financial products—the flavor of the day, as I like to call them—but most advisers and brokers, I believe, act like Switzerland: they are neutral and will let you sell and buy whatever you want, even if it's not in your best interest. Even if you're rational, it's coming from a place of greed or fear. It is at these very times, when both elements are present, that it's most dangerous for you and your portfolio's long-term financial health.

When emotion sets in, a wealth coach will help you not fall prey to these self-destructive decisions. These are the times when I really earn my fees. It's not hard to sit with clients when their portfolio is up 12 percent, but it takes a different skill set on both sides of the conference table to help these same people when the portfolio is down 20 percent or more. A good coach stands for something or ultimately stands for nothing! I would rather lose a client than sit idly by and even profit by my ongoing fees by allowing them to do something that I believe is not in his or her best interest and is emotionally driven.

Remember that a well-designed portfolio is systematically engineered with many different ingredients, like a great meal. It's simply not a collection of historically well-performing investments. The best ingredients in the kitchen can create the worst meal ever if all you do is throw them in one pot and hope it works.

Get Organized

• • •

I'M NOT SURE HOW YOU and your ex ran your home, but it was my responsibility to find or hire all the necessary contractors to help maintain our home. It became very clear to me that my ex-wife didn't know who handled our homes day to day maintenance issues. She would call me often with questions like:

- Who handles our heating and air conditioning?
- When were the filters changed last?

- Who do we use to clean our gutters?
- Who plows the snow?
- Who's our electrician and plumber?

These are just some of the important and common questions that every divorcée needs the answers to. With that in mind, I have included a simple guide to help you stay organized as you run your new world.

Name and phone numbers:
Plumber_____
Electrician _____
Gutter service_____
Exterminator_____
Landscaper_____
Lawn-fertilizer company_____
Attorney_____
CPA_____
Septic service_____
Tree service_____
Garage-door company_____
Snow-removal service_____
Roofer_____
Safety-deposit-box location and number_____
Insurance agents:
Life insurance_____
Health insurance_____
Auto insurance_____

CONCLUSION

• • •

MAYBE THE CONCEPT $1 + 1 = 2$ is all around us. Believing that $1 + 1 = 2$ makes our world seem more manageable and easy to understand. We want things to be simple and easy to deal with, so we can move on to the next task. We want to be able to believe what we read and see or hear on the six o'clock news. I hate to break the bad news to you, but life doesn't always work that way. There are so many groups out there today with such self-serving motivations to convince you that $1 + 1 = 2.$ You, the consumer, can't just settle for what appears to be the obvious, and you must probe deeper with your questions and conduct research so you can uncover your own "*maybe.*"

I have a few simple questions for you:

1. Do you let past performance of an investment cloud your future investment decisions?
2. Do you think that it would be important for you to know what you are really paying in all fees, not just advisory fees?
3. Is it important for you to determine if your portfolio is too risky? And I am not just referring to the percentage of equity in your portfolio allocation.

4. Would it make more sense to manage your portfolio with a systematic strategy, with regard to when and how to rebalance, that is 100 percent free from emotion?
5. Do you think it would help you if you had an investment philosophy that is constant and something you can rely on in both good and bad times, which is 100 percent free from emotion?
6. Do you spend too much time watching and listening to TV and radio shows about investments?
7. Do you rely on a lot of online calculators, your custodian's research, financial magazines, newsletters, and websites to make your decisions?
8. Do you worry that there may not be enough money to create the retirement lifestyle you hope for?
9. Do you wish you understood investing more?
10. Has this book helped you look at investing a little differently?

If you answered yes too many of these questions, you are like the hundreds of other divorcées who have come to my office looking for answers and peace of mind.

I hope that you have enjoyed this short book; but more importantly, I hope that it spurs you to action and learn more.

If you are in the Akron, Ohio, area, we would love to meet with you and do an analysis of your portfolio, 401(k), IRA, or current or future divorce settlement. This will help give you a more comprehensive understanding of what's really happening with your investments and help you achieve greater peace of mind and confidence as an investor.

If you are outside the Akron, Ohio, area, we can offer an online portfolio analysis as well.

For a wide variety of free reports, go to http://www.leehyder.com, and click on "Free reports."

If you wish to attend our next divorcée survival boot camp, contact me personally by e-mail (lee@leehyder.com), or call 330-836-7800.

www.ingramcontent.com/pod-product-compliance
Lightning Source LLC
Chambersburg PA
CBHW050015230526
45470CB00003B/975